God Made Only One Me

Dear Parents and Teachers:

Understanding that God made each of us different from one another can help children accept themselves and each other. They see that it is acceptable to be different; in fact, it is God's plan that each person be one of a kind. This book shows how to resolve personality clashes with others. It also encourages children to ask God to help them change their behavior if they are offensive to others.

Gail Robinson

Verses marked TLB are taken from THE LIVING BIBLE, © 1971 by Tyndale House Publishers, Wheaton, IL. Used by permission.

Copyright © 1986 Concordia Publishing House
3558 S. Jefferson Avenue, St. Louis, MO   63118-3968
Manufactured in the United States of America

Library of Congress Cataloging in Publication Data

Robinson, Gail, 1944–
        God made only one me.

        Summary: Indicates that individuals should understand how they were all made to be unique in personality and that they can turn to God for help and support when change is needed in interacting with others.
        1. Children—Religious life. 2. Self-acceptance—Religious aspects—Christianity—Juvenile literature. 3. Interpersonal relations—Religious aspects—Christianity—Juvenile literature. [1. Self-perception. 2. Christian life] I. Mattozzi, Patricia, ill. II. Title.
BV4571.2.R63   1986   248.8'2   86-12903
ISBN 0-570-04148-1

1 2 3 4 5 6 7 8 9 10 DP 95 94 93 92 91 90 89 88 87 86

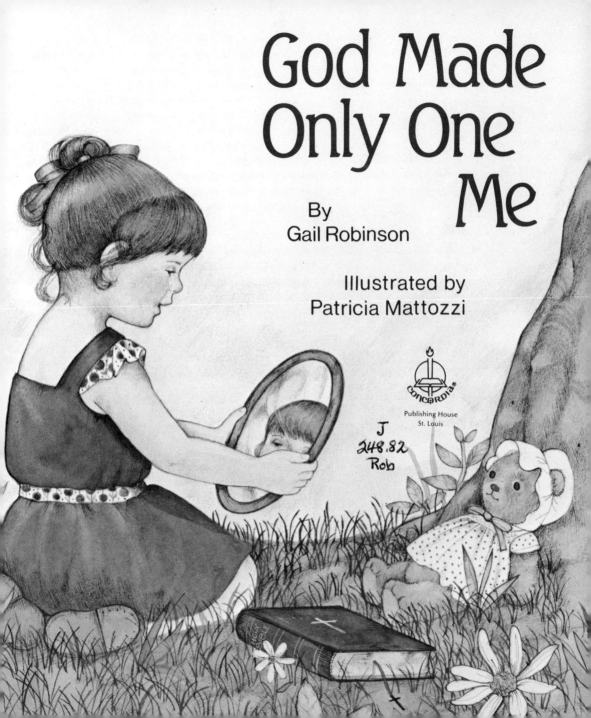

God Made Only One Me

By
Gail Robinson

Illustrated by
Patricia Mattozzi

CONCORDIA®

Publishing House
St. Louis

Thank you for making me so wonderfully complex! It is amazing to think about. Your workmanship is marvelous—and how well I know it.

Psalm 139:14 TLB

Maybe I'm shy, or maybe I'm not.
Maybe I giggle and wiggle a lot.
Maybe I've always my nose in a book,
Or like to catch fish with a worm on my hook.
I'm thankful, O God, that You made me, me.
Your plan is the best; that's easy to see.

How I feel, how I act, and what I like and dislike, are all part of what makes me, ME. People call that *personality*. God made all of us different on the outside. He also made us different on the inside, where we think and feel.

My friend, Karen, loves to ride on a roller coaster. Not me! I get scared and scoot way down in my seat. I close my eyes tight until the ride is over. Sometimes my tummy hurts when I get off. Karen laughs and says, "Let's go again!" God made us different.

Jason and Jared are brothers. Jared likes to play baseball better than anything. Jason would rather read a book instead. He doesn't like sports. Even though they are brothers, God made Jason and Jared different.

Even when people are different, they can be friends. Because God loves many different kinds of people and is their Friend, I can be their friend, too.

Clark, a new boy in my class, seemed strange to the rest of us until we got to know him. At recess he often stays in the classroom to read. He uses big words and asks the teacher lots of questions.

At first we laughed at Clark. But soon he became our friend. Now we all want him on our spelling team.

School is more interesting because God made teachers different, too. My teacher, Mr. Brant, talks loud and laughs a lot. He loves to tell jokes. When he does tell a joke, he laughs louder than anyone.

Mrs. Lacey, my teacher last year, is different from Mr. Brant. Her voice is soft. She talks slowly and pats us on the shoulder. When she laughs, it is more like a chuckle.

Because we are not perfect, our personalities sometimes get us into trouble. Jeffrey loves to tell stories. At school everyone likes to sit at his table to hear his new jokes and stories. One day Jeff was telling us about a fire at his neighbor's house. I knew he wasn't telling the exact truth because I saw the fire, too. Jeff didn't mean to lie. He wanted everyone to like his story, so he made up things to make it more exciting. Telling a lie is wrong. Jeff should stick to the truth.

Jennifer, my best friend, always wants to be the leader. She is a good leader, too. At recess, she knows the best way to divide everyone into teams. She thinks up exciting games for us to play.

But sometimes I get tired of Jennifer always being the leader. Just once I'd like to be the leader and give the orders.

My other friends leave when Jennifer orders them around. They call her "bossy." I tell her, "Jennifer, you'd have more friends if you didn't order everyone around."

"I know," Jennifer says, "but how can I change the way I am?"

"If you ask God, He will help you to change," I say.

My brothers, Kevin and Kyle, share a room. Kevin makes his bed every morning and hangs up his clothes. His toys and books are always put back on the shelf when he finishes with them.

Kevin is the kind of person who likes everything in its place.

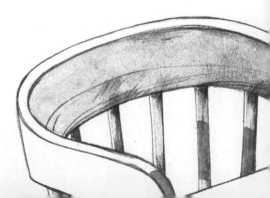

Kyle doesn't even notice how messy the room is until Mom says, "Get this room cleaned up, NOW!"

Then he puts away his clothes and pushes in his drawers. It takes him a long time because he looks out the window. He plays with his model cars while he's putting them away.

Kyle is the kind of person who daydreams a lot and doesn't care if his room is a mess.

God made both Kevin and Kyle, and even though they are different, He loves them both.

Kyle and Kevin fight a lot because one of them is messy and the other is neat. Sometimes they even hit each other.

Kevin and Kyle can get along, if they try. Each one must give in a little. They can ask God to help them get along better.

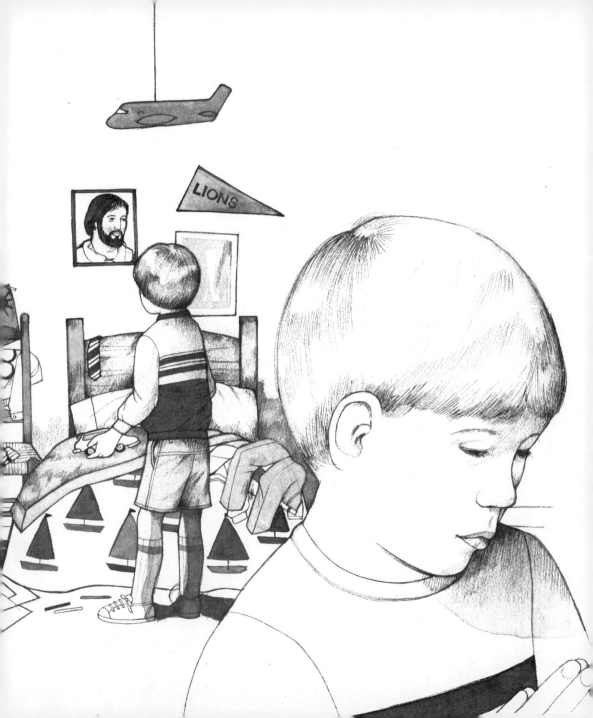

Kevin could pray, "Jesus, help me not to scream at Kyle when he stuffs his dirty socks under the bed."

Kyle could pray, "Help me to keep my room neat. I know it's important to my brother."

It will take a while, but God will help them change.

How did God make you? Are you full of questions like Clark, or neat like Kevin? Perhaps you are loud and jolly like Mr. Brant, or quiet and gentle like Mrs. Lacey. Whatever you are like, there is no other person in the world just like you.

A Prayer

Thank You, God for making only one me. It makes me feel special. Thank You, too, for helping me get along with others who are different from me. If there is something about me that needs to changed, like being too bossy or stretching the truth, forgive me because of Jesus and then help me to change. In Jesus' name I pray. Amen.